The Skinny on Real Estate Investing

the skinny on™

real estate investing

an introduction
to the subject

Jim Randel

ISBN: 978-0-9818935-6-3
Illustration: Malinda Nass ☺

For information address RAND Publishing, 265 Post Road West, Westport, CT, 06880 or call (203) 226-8727.

The Skinny On™ books are available for special promotions and premiums. For details contact: Donna Hardy, call (203) 222-6295 or visit our website: www.theskinnyon.com

Printed in the United States of America

the skinny on™

Welcome to a new series of publications entitled **The Skinny On**™, a progression of drawings, dialogue and text intended to convey information in a concise fashion.

In our time-starved and information-overloaded culture, most of us have far too little time to read and absorb major important writings and research on important topics. So, our understanding tends to float on the surface – without the benefit of the thinking of the writers and teachers who have spent years studying these topics.

Our series is intended to address this situation. Our team of readers and researchers has done a ton of homework in preparing our books for you. We have read just about everything respected author on a particular topic and distilled what we learned into this "skinny" book for your benefit.

You might think of our book as concentrated learning. By spending one or two hours reading our book, we maintain that you get the benefit of the hundreds of hours you would spend reading all the works on a particular subject.

Our goal is to do the reading for you, cull out what is important, distill the key points and present them in a book that we hope is both instructive and entertaining.

Although minimalist in design, we do take our message very seriously. Please do not confuse format with content. The time you invest reading this book will be paid back to you many, many times over.

AUTHOR'S NOTE

I am really excited about writing this book. I have been an active real estate investor for thirty years. I have bought and sold single-family houses, small multi-family properties, apartment complexes, retail centers, office buildings, factories, warehouses and land.

I have had some terrific successes. I have also had some huge failures. I am hoping that I can give you a framework to mirror my successes and avoid my flops.

In 2006 I wrote a book about my career as an investor, *Confessions of a Real Estate Entrepreneur* (McGraw Hill). I was honored when Robert Bruss, a highly-respected columnist, rated *Confessions* "a 12...on a scale of 1 to 10!" In that book I speak to the good deals I did ... and also the mistakes.

And, I have been a guest speaker at business schools (Harvard and NYU), at annual realtor conventions (NAR, Re/Max) and at investor clubs around the country.

I have two goals with this book:

1) To introduce you to the subject of real estate investing and give you a feel for how a real estate investor makes his or her living.

2) To disabuse the notion that real estate investing is a "get rich quick" scenario. I hate the promoters who play on people's dreams by selling "get rich quick" schemes. In my thirty years in the business I have seen lots of real estate investors get very rich <u>but</u>, it usually wasn't quick, <u>and</u> it was never easy!

The opportunities are out there for you and I am going to try to help you identify them. But, if you are thinking quick and easy money, don't buy this book!

"Hi, my name is Jim Randel and I am going to be telling you the story of Billy and Beth, a nice young couple who want to better themselves financially.

Unfortunately, they are susceptible to the devices of clever marketers who sell seminars and products promoting real estate investing as a quick, 'risk-free' path to wealth."

SAY "HELLO" TO BILLY AND BETH.

4

"Beth, look at this e-mail from a guy who makes $20,000 a month owning real estate ... he works just weekends and uses very little of his own money! He has invited me to attend a seminar he is giving. And it is totally free."

5

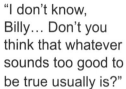

"I started with no money. Then I discovered a fool-proof strategy for buying and flipping real estate. In no time, I owned 12 houses and had $20,000 coming in each and every month."

Real Estate
Money Makers
Seminar

"YES! I want some of that."

8

"And so you shall, my friend. We here at Real Estate Money Makers want to share our secrets with you. So we have prepared a Money Makers System – 8 CDs and a workbook – that is available exclusively to attendees at this conference.

"The retail value of this offering is $1,200 but for those of you who buy today, and today only, the price is only $399!!"

9

Billy envisioning himself as "Guess Who?".

10

Something tells me that whatever is in that bag was not free.

Real Estate Money Makers

11

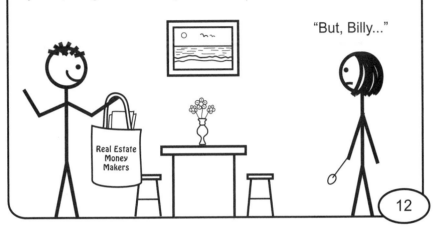

"Beth, it was terrific. There are many strategies I can learn that will make us lots of extra money investing in real estate. And there is a money-back guarantee. If we do not double our net worth within two years, we get our money back."

"But, Billy..."

Real Estate Money Makers

12

"And listen to this, Beth. Next month Real Estate Money Makers is having a boot camp for beginners. If I register today, it is only $2,000!"

"But, Billy…"

Real Estate Money Makers

13

"Beth ... I feel really good about this ... real estate is the safest investment you can make."

Real Estate Money Makers

BUT JIM IS CONCERNED.

"Why did this have to have to happen on the day of my first solo sky-dive?"

16

17

"I hate promoters who downplay the risk, time and effort that is required to make money with real estate. I just don't want you to sign on to something and then be disappointed."

"Would you like a cup of coffee?"

22

"Yes, thank you … and some aspirin please."

"Next time call first."

23

24

25

"The key to all real estate investing is understanding what is called a cash-flow analysis. The logic of this analysis is the same whether you are buying a single-family house or a huge shopping center. The larger the property, the more numbers you need to review, but the methodology is the same.

"To start, let's analyze a house that happens to be for sale down the street from you. The asking price is $275,000. I checked around and found that if it were for lease it would rent for about $2,500 a month with the tenant paying all utilities.

"The question is whether this house makes sense as a real estate investment."

"But, Jim, do single-family houses sell on an investment analysis? Aren't people who are going to live in a house usually willing to pay more than an investor would?"

"That is a really great question, Beth."

"Historically, most homebuyers did not analyze a house as an investment. They just bought, assuming prices would always go up. But prices did not keep rising, and today we have a lot of homes worth less than they were worth just 2 or 3 years ago."

"Jim, all the financial advisors were telling people that the best investment one could make was to buy their own home. So Beth and I bought our house without even thinking about its rental value."

"I know that, Billy, and one of my gripes with real estate authors and speakers is that they did not explain the risk that house values could just as easily go down as go up."

29

"The philosophy behind the automatic millionaire homeowner

- *You can't get rich renting.*
- *You don't need a lot of money for a down payment on a home.*
- *You don't need good credit to buy a home.*
- *You should buy a home even if you have credit card debt.*

...

You're about to enter the world of homeownership and real estate investing, a world that is far easier to understand – and to conquer – than you ever imagined."

The Automatic Millionaire Homeowner, David Bach (Broadway Books, 2005)

30

Note that soon after this book was published, home prices started a long downward spiral. Anyone who bought in 2005 has probably lost +/-25% of the value of their purchase. Some experts believe that house prices could fall another 10% – 20%. If homebuyers in 2005 had done a cash-flow analysis instead of banking on price increases, their house would at least make sense as an investment property.

Why do I go after Mr. Bach? Because I feel that too many well-established financial writers jumped on the real estate bandwagon without giving people an adequate explanation of the risks.

31

"By the way, I have made more than my share of mistakes too.

"If you want to read about some of the really dumb real estate investing stuff I have done, e-mail me and I will send you, free of charge, a copy of Chapter 9 from my book, *Confessions of a Real Estate Entrepreneur*. This chapter was written to help others avoid making the same dumb mistakes I made."

jrandel@theskinnyon.com

32

I do believe that homeownership is a great investment for most people.

I just want potential home buyers to understand that there is risk … and that performing a cash-flow analysis of a prospective purchase should be at least part of the thinking as to the price to pay.

*"In the first few years of the (21st century), Americans' long fixation with home owning metastasized into the biggest residential real estate bubble in history. Meanwhile the home-owning cultural mania prevailed … telling you that every dollar you spend on your home is worth more than a dollar in the bank or in government bonds or in the stock market … Home owning, went much of the bubble era's conventional wisdom, was the one financial sure thing. **Get real. Home owning is not now, was not then and never has been a guaranteed moneymaker.**"*

The Wall Street Journal Complete Homeowners Guidebook,
David Crook (Three Rivers Press, 2008)

33

"OK, let's get back to our analysis of the house down the street.

"The question is this: Does the asking price of $275,000 make sense if the house has a rental value of $2,500 per month, which is $30,000/year?"

34

ANNUAL GROSS RENTS: $30,000

ANNUAL EXPENSES:
Real Estate Taxes: $6,000
Insurance: $3,000
Maintenance: $2,000
Miscellaneous: + $500

Total: $11,500 $11,500

NET OPERATING INCOME: $18,500

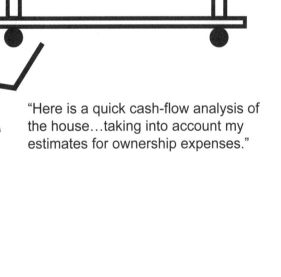

"Here is a quick cash-flow analysis of the house…taking into account my estimates for ownership expenses."

"Note that I have used a new term, 'net operating income.' This is a really important concept in the real estate investing world. It means all revenues minus all expenses. Oftentimes it is abbreviated to NOI."

38

"As you can see, the proposed NOI from this house is $18,500. Assuming that number is correct, do you think the house is worth $275,000?"

"Well, $18,500 over $275,000 is about a 6.7% annual return on investment…not too bad."

39

40

41

While Jim is resting, let's recap what we have learned so far:

1. Prices that go up can also come down. Even home-buyers planning to live in a house may want to consider an investment analysis when determining the price to pay.

2. Whether analyzing the purchase of a single-family house or a large shopping center, the methodology of analysis is the same. The bigger the property the more numbers to factor in, but the type of calculation does not really change.

3. The starting point for all investment analyses is Net Operating Income (or NOI) which is revenues (rents) minus ownership expenses.

THE NEXT DAY

"Yesterday I mentioned that investors like to 'add value' to real estate. We are going to talk more about that but first I want to tell you about an 'added value' deal I did. My partner and I bought an old factory and turned it into a factory outlet mall."

"Without changing the building at all, we were able to add millions of dollars of value to the property with a new leasing approach. Adding value simply means finding ways to increase the value of your property by multiples of whatever you invest. If you invest one dollar, you hope to increase the value of your property by five dollars."

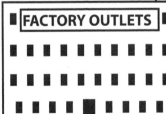

FACTORY OUTLETS

"One thing we did not factor in yesterday was financing. Unless you have a spare $275,000 lying around, you are going to need to get a mortgage to buy the house. Billy, do you want to take a stab at calculating what financing does to our analysis?"

"What kind of loop brings a blackboard into a diner?"

"Well, to buy that house we would need to get a mortgage for about 80% of the purchase price… or about $220,000. And I think we can get a mortgage at a 6.5% interest rate, interest only for a couple of years."

80% of the purchase price = $220,000

• Mortgage: 6.5%

"OK, let's assume you are correct. What does that do to our analysis?"

"Well, our NOI is $18,500 and now we have to deduct from that the interest we would pay on our $220,000 mortgage. 6.5% times $220,000 equals $14,300 per year. So, now our net income is $4,200 per year."

$18,500 NOI
− $14,300 interest
$4,200 per year

"Well done, Billy. But that $4,200 is usually called 'cash flow'…essentially the money remaining after expenses and debt service."

"You have mentioned risk a lot. This kind of a purchase seems pretty straightforward ... what can go wrong?"

"Wow, Beth... it's almost as if you read my mind... let's talk about risk!"

The problem with inexperienced real estate investors is that they almost always underestimate what can go wrong with a deal. They get all excited about doing a deal and they get swept away with thinking about all the good stuff that can happen. An intelligent investor needs to consider both the good and the bad.

The smart real estate investor is not afraid of risk. He or she understands that risk is part of the game. The smart real estate investor is prepared to take <u>calculated risks</u> – risks that make sense when one considers the potential upside of a deal and the probability of bad things happening.

59

"Anyone who has been investing in real estate for any period of time knows that <u>what can go wrong</u> often <u>will go wrong</u> and that success with real estate requires you to: (1) try to think of everything that can go wrong, and (2) make sure that your return on investment is high enough to compensate for the possibility of bad things happening."

60

"Here are just some of the things that could go wrong:

1. The house could be harder to lease than anticipated.
2. The rent we have projected may be too high.
3. There may be physical problems with the house that you did not uncover during an inspection.
4. You may get deadbeat tenants who don't pay rent and trash the house.
5. It could cost you lots of time and money to evict bad tenants.
6. The town may create rent-control laws.
7. Your neighbor's tree may fall on your house. Although the repair will probably be covered by insurance, your tenant may have a right to break his lease.
8. Someone could parachute onto your roof and dent it!

Do you want me to go on?"

64

65

"Jim, given your desire for that return, if we were going to buy the house to rent out, what should we pay for it?"

"Just give me a minute ... well, if you pay $235,000 with an 80% mortgage, your cash flow will be about $6,300 over capital invested of $47,000, and the return will be 13.4% a year. At that number I am interested."

66

"That is ridiculous, Jim. The asking price is $275,000. They are not going to take a price of $235,000."

"Great, Billy, then we have just learned Lesson Number 1 about real estate investing. If the seller does not want to take your offer, walk away... you need to learn to walk away. An asking price is a meaningless number."

67

68

69

"But before I do that, let me ask you something. Why do you want to invest in real estate? Is it just to make money?"

"Yeah, that's pretty much it."

70

"That's what I was afraid you would say. So, I have to make one other very important point. Investing in real estate is not like buying stocks or bonds which are totally passive investments. Real estate is an active investment. You need to deal with tenants, with lenders, with brokers and lawyers, with zoning and building departments, and so on."

"And your point is?"

71

"My point is that to be very successful at real estate investing – or perhaps at anything for that matter – you really have to enjoy the process. If you are just driven to make money, if that is all that motivates you, I am worried for your success. In fact, if you will allow me, I would like to tell you a story."

"Is it long?"

"Ignore him, Jim … I'd like to hear it."

"I grew up in a very small town, Perkins Township, Ohio. There was not much going on in Perkins. No stores. No gas station. Not even a stop light. In fact there was just one large building – an armory where the Ohio National Guard would have meetings. And, on occasion, there would be events in the armory, like 4-H tractor pulls and concerts."

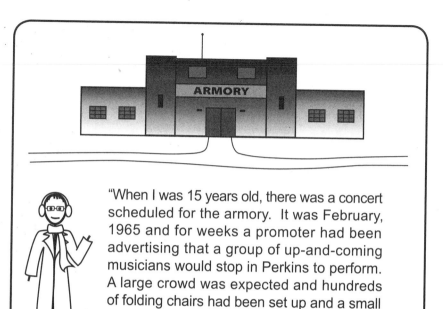

"When I was 15 years old, there was a concert scheduled for the armory. It was February, 1965 and for weeks a promoter had been advertising that a group of up-and-coming musicians would stop in Perkins to perform. A large crowd was expected and hundreds of folding chairs had been set up and a small stage erected."

74

"The problem began about 6 PM. The musicians had arrived and were unloading their equipment when it began to snow. And I mean SNOW. Huge flakes falling like crazy. Within an hour the roads were impassable. No one could get to the armory except me and a couple of my farm-boy buddies who lived nearby and could walk there."

75

"We were the only ones inside and we could sit wherever we wanted. We had never sat anywhere near the front before and of course we selected the first row. We were very excited!"

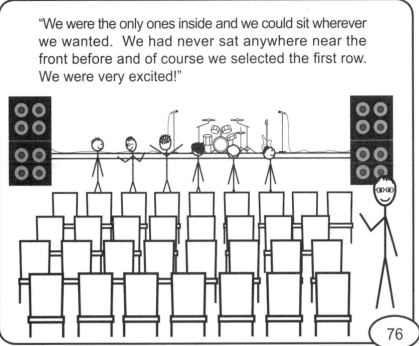

"But the musicians were very disappointing. It was obvious that they wanted to be anywhere but Perkins Township and they could not get off the stage fast enough. They went through the motions of performing their song and then rushed off the stage."

"Until the last performer. He was a young Welshman named Tom Jones and he had just released a new song called 'What's New Pussycat?' To our surprise he actually spoke to us."

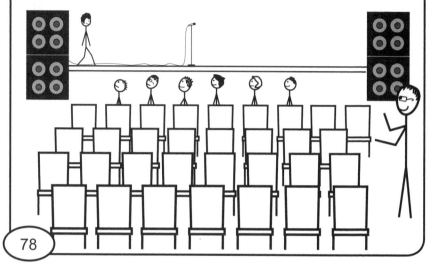

"I am very disappointed by the snow storm. But I want to thank those of you who were able to get here for showing up. And I hope you will remember my song."

"What's new pussycat? Whoa whoa whoaaaa!"

"And Tom Jones belted out 'What's New Pussycat?' like he was in Las Vegas performing in front of thousands. And in the empty armory, there was nothing to deaden the sound and the place shook!! We gave him a standing ovation, and he smiled and left the stage."

"And that night as I was making my way home, it hit me: success is about finding something you are really passionate about and doing it to the best of your ability. Tom Jones loved to perform. He was unhappy that there were so few people in the audience of course, but he still did his best and sang like he was in front of thousands."

"I realized that evening that I needed to identify what I was passionate about and go for it. I have never forgotten what I learned that evening in 1965 – that if you find something you really love doing, you will eventually do well and bring yourself lots of pleasure in the process."

82

"By the way, Tom Jones has gone on from Perkins, Ohio to have a long and amazing career with many hit songs. At age 70 he has just released a new album and he is currently performing to large crowds all around the world."

83

OK, TIME TO GET UP. STRETCH YOUR LEGS. SING A LITTLE "WHAT'S NEW PUSSYCAT?" OR, ANY SONG FOR THAT MATTER. TOO MUCH READING CAN MAKE YOUR BRAIN GO SOFT.

OR HAVE A LITTLE SNACK. BUT PLEASE COME BACK.

I'M TRYING TO RAP, BUT I'M REALLY JUST A SAP.

OK, before we go back to Billy and Beth, let me tell you three points about real estate investing:

1. Good real estate investors enjoy the physical over the metaphysical. Some people love sifting through stock charts, economic data, and financial reports. Others are more experiential and want to see tangible evidence of their investments. The latter are usually better real estate investors than the former (but the former are better chess players).

2. Good salespeople do well at it. Real estate investing, in a nutshell, is about procuring property and then leasing it to others. The analysis part of it is really not that hard. What is hard is finding and obtaining the real estate (dealing with sellers, brokers and lenders) and then leasing it to individuals or businesses (dealing with all sorts of people and/or their advisors).

3. To be a good real estate investor you must be a comfortable (but judicious) risk taker. Real estate investing is risky. You not only commit your own money to a venture but usually a lot of borrowed money for which you are personally responsible (i.e. you have to pay it back even if the real estate deal goes sour). If you are risk-adverse, real estate investing is probably not for you.

And now, back to our story ...

91

92

93

94

"A co-worker of mine just inherited a small retail building in town. I heard him talking about selling it and I was curious as to what you would think about our putting in an offer?"

"Well, Beth, just like the analysis of the house down the street, we need to do a cash-flow analysis and figure out what the property is worth. Can you ask your co-worker for the numbers on the property?"

"I already did that Jim."

"Great, Beth…you know lots of times the best deals are those you learn about by word of mouth…let's look at the numbers."

"Square footage is a big deal in the real estate world. A square foot is a square that measures one foot by one foot. Everything in investment real estate is tied to square footage. The size of a building, the rent per square foot, the sales price per square foot … and so on."

"Beth, what you have given me is called a Pro Forma. It is a written outline of the property's income and expenses. What I take from this Pro Forma is that the building has four leasable spaces, each about 1,250 square feet, one of which is vacant. The rent from the existing three tenants is $100,000 per year and the operating expenses are $35,000 ... leaving us with a net operating income of $65,000."

101

"Well, presuming your co-worker wants to sell this property, you might make an offer."

"I understand, Jim, but what do we do next?"

102

"How do we know what to offer?"

"I now need to tell you about something called a 'cap rate'."

103

"Some investors use a 'cap rate', which is short for capitalization rate, to get a quick sense of what they will pay for a property.

"A cap rate is usually between 5% and 15%. It represents the return an investor would expect on his capital if he bought a property with no financing."

104

"No worries guys … this is a little confusing at first.

"So let's stick with our example. Let's say we are feeling fairly optimistic about the economy and that because we like the location of this building and its potential to attract tenants, we will accept an annual return of 8% on our capital. Therefore, we will pay a price for this building which will generate that yield, and the way to determine that price is to divide our net operating income of $65,000 by 8%."

Here is
the math:

105

106

NET OPERATING INCOME = $65,000

Desired Return on
Capital (CAP RATE) =   8%

MATH: $65,000/.08 = $812,500

SO, WE WILL PAY $812,500 FOR THE PROPERTY.

"The math skills needed to be a good real estate investor are not complicated. **We are not talking brain surgery!**"

AS IT HAPPENS, BILLY'S COUSIN, MELVIN, IS A BRAIN SURGEON ... BUT DEFINITELY NOT BEST OF CLASS.

"Oops!"

"Here is what it says about cap rates in *Confessions of a Real Estate Entrepreneur*:

'A cap rate is the rate that a purchaser would be willing to receive as a return on its cash to own a particular property. Cap rates go up and down as the economy strengthens or weakens, as interest rates go up and down, and as the investor community perceives the safety (or not) of a specific piece of property. Different types of properties generally fetch different cap rates'."

111

"Wow, I'm flattered that you bought my book."

"Well, actually I took it out of the library."

112

"Well I'm flattered nevertheless."

"Jim, I'm still confused. Why would you use an 8% cap rate when you have said that you will never do a deal unless it will deliver a 10% – 12% per year return on your equity?"

113

"Good question, Beth. But, think again about my analysis ... are you really going to earn only an 8% return? Or, are there opportunities for you to add value to this deal?"

114

"Are the two of you forgetting that there is a vacant space in the building? I have checked around and that space should rent for $25 per square foot plus utilities. Since adding another tenant to the building will not increase operating expenses, if you can lease that space, you will immediately increase the net operating income of the property by $31,250."

117

"Ah, I see that you are still a little confused. I forgot to explain a step or two. As I mentioned, everything in real estate investing comes down to dollars per square foot. When rent is quoted at $25 per square foot, annual rent for a particular space is calculated by multiplying $25 times the amount of square footage. Since the building we are analyzing has a vacant space of 1,250 square feet, if you can rent it, you will drop $31,250 right to your bottom line."

$$
\begin{array}{r}
1{,}250 \text{ SF} \\
\times\ \$25/\text{SF} \\
\hline
\$31{,}250
\end{array}
$$

118

"Excellent, Beth, you are exactly right."

I was just about to say the same thing.

121

"Earlier I had said that you should only buy an investment property if you can earn a minimum of 10% – 12% on your investment. But that may not be the return from day one. You may have to add value to what you buy – just as we are discussing leasing up the vacant space in the retail property. However, if you can't earn an annual return of 10% – 12% on your investment fairly early into a deal, then you should not buy it. There are just too many things that can go wrong."

122

The way to make money investing in real estate is to find deals where you can ADD VALUE. By that I mean you have an opportunity to do something which enhances net operating income quickly. Here are some examples of how to add value to a property:

1. Lease vacant space.

2. Reposition the property – improve image from B to A and obtain higher rents.

3. Renovate the property – improve appearance – more attractive buildings earn higher rents.

4. Change the use of the property – from a low rent use to a higher rent use.

5. Increase the size of the property.

And so on. The logic in all cases is to find some way to boost the rent roll of the property (or cut expenses) so that more money falls to the bottom line, i.e., you increase net operating income. And you attempt to do so in a way which increases your return on equity quickly and dramatically.

I do not subscribe to a non-entrepreneurial theory of real estate investing which ASSUMES that over time rents will increase and so will values. That is, to me, much higher risk than an "added value" approach.

For one thing, rents do not always go up. Across the country, the successful deals I have seen are those where an investor did not depend on inflation or gradual rent increases to boost his or her net operating income.

A good real estate entrepreneur does not wait for appreciation but rather takes the bull by the horns in a proactive effort to increase value.

"You see the great thing about real estate investing, as distinguished from stock or bonds or annuities or money markets, is that you CAN INFLUENCE the outcome of your investment."

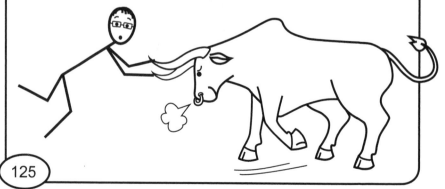

"When you buy a stock or bond or other passive investment, you sit and wait for external forces to push the price of your investment one way or another. Not so with real estate."

AND NOW, BACK TO BILLY AND BETH

"So, if you can lease the vacant space, you will boost your return on equity to almost 12%. That is an example of adding value."

"But won't the owner of the property know that too? Why doesn't he just rent the space, and then offer the property with a higher net income?"

"Well, Beth, I presume that if he could easily do that, he would have done so already. Perhaps he is not using the right broker … or, the space doesn't show well. Many sellers miss opportunities to enhance value, and that is why entrepreneurial real estate investors can make a lot of money."

"Maybe there are costs to renting the vacant space and he does not want to incur those expenses."

"Hey, Billy, now you are adding value to our discussion. Well done!"

130

"Let's assume that it will cost you $20,000 in leasing fees and down time to lease the vacant space. If you can convince the seller to sell for $812,500 and assuming $20,000 in lease-up expenses and another $10,000 in closing costs, is this still a good deal?"

"I would say, yes. Our projected NOI is $96,250 and our investment with the additional $30,000 will be $842,500... still about an 11.4% unleveraged return on our capital. Not bad."

131

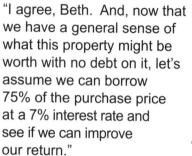

"I agree, Beth. And, now that we have a general sense of what this property might be worth with no debt on it, let's assume we can borrow 75% of the purchase price at a 7% interest rate and see if we can improve our return."

"Jim, I would like to take a stab at doing the math."

132

"Great. Go for it, Billy!"

133

"Well, if we can get a loan of 75% of the purchase price of $812,500, then we can borrow $609,375. If the interest rate is 7%, interest only for the first few years, our debt service is about $42,700. Since our NOI is $96,250, we will have a cash flow of $53,550. With leasing expenses of $20,000 and closing costs of $10,000, we need $233,000 to do this deal. So our return on equity is $53,550 divided by $233,000 or about 23% per year!"

134

"Well done, Billy. Good analysis and right on the money ... no pun intended!"

135

"We have no idea what Beth's work friend will sell his property for. But, if he has not been able to rent the vacant space and you think you can, this may be a great opportunity for you."

"The reason some real estate investors make so much money is that they execute where others cannot or will not. Here, the opportunity for adding value is the difference between the seller's inability to lease the vacant space and Billy and Beth's ability to do so. That gap is hugely important!!"

"One problem, Jim. We don't have anywhere near the $233,000 needed to buy and lease this property."

138

"Well, Beth, like many beginning real estate investors, you have to be creative at finding money. For one thing you might be able to convince the seller to take back a second mortgage for some of the money."

139

"But for now let's assume that he cannot or will not do that. For that reason, I want to introduce you to what is sometimes called syndication.

"Syndication is just a big word for raising money to acquire an asset. It means nothing more than finding partners who want to invest with you.

"Let's assume that Beth's co-worker is willing to sell for $812,500 and you need to come up with $233,000. I will presume that you can come up with $35,000 and so you need to raise about $200,000. Let's strategize how you might do that.

"I'm sure you know some people looking to invest money if they can earn an excellent return. You offer them an interest in the entity you are going to form to buy this property.

"The most common form of ownership is a limited liability company, or 'LLC'. The owners of the LLC are 'members' and you can structure the LLC so that different members have differing responsibilities and returns."

"As the people who created this deal, you are the ones who should run it, what are called the 'managers' of the LLC.

"As the managers, you should earn a fee for the services you provide in running the deal. Since you created the deal and are signing for the loan (the investors usually do not), I suggest $10,000 per year. In addition, you should set aside an annual reserve of say $5,000 for unexpected expenses.

"Subtracting these sums from the projected cash flow of $53,550, you still have $38,550 to distribute. So, given total investment capital of $233,000, the investors will receive a 16.5% annual return. This includes your $35,000 of course.

"Some real estate entrepreneurs would structure the distributions more favorably to themselves. For example, they might provide that after all invested capital receives a 10% annual return, all excess income goes 70% to the entrepreneur and 30% to the investors. The investors still receive a very competitive return and the people who create the deal do very, very well."

"With a 16.5% potential return, you should be able to attract investors. So you will have a deal which is paying you a manager's fee of $10,000 per year and a nice return on your own investment. In addition, this deal will help you build a reputation as smart real estate investors."

142

"This may help clarify the numbers ... I had Fido go get a written analysis I did."

143

Gross Rent:	$131,250
Operating Expenses:	− $35,000
Net Operating Income =	$96,250
Debt Service (interest):	− $42,700
CASH FLOW:	$53,550
Manager's Fee:	− $10,000
Reserve:	− $5,000
Cash Available for Distribution:	$38,550
Annual Return on Partners' Capital ($38,550/$233,000) =	16.5%

"Jim, is doing a deal and raising money really this easy?"

"Beth, I do not want to give you the impression that any of this is EASY. Real estate investing can be very, very lucrative but it does require hard work, persistence and salesmanship.

"I am giving you just the basics today and will be coming back for more visits (look for *The Skinny on Real Estate Investing, Part II)*. For now I just want to introduce you to the whole idea of investing. For me it has been a wonderful, profitable career. Perhaps it can be for you too!"

"Well, I have to be going now... I hope to see you again soon."

"Thanks, Jim."

"My goal with Billy and Beth was to introduce them to the idea of real estate investing. In some cases I have simplified the numbers. For example, I have assumed that they could obtain interest-only loans although most loans require that in addition to interest, a borrower pay down principal every month. Still, those amounts won't change the analysis much.

"I have also glossed over the mechanics of leasing space, of analyzing the appropriate market rents for a vacant space and the details of a closing. All of that will be addressed in future books.

"I hope that this book will help you decide whether real estate investing sounds like an activity you would enjoy. As with all our books, please feel free to come to our website with your questions. We look forward to hearing from you."

www.theskinnyon.com

"Good for Billy and Beth!!!"

"I hope that you have enjoyed this Introduction to Real Estate Investing. In the next few pages I summarize for you the 10 most important points to take from this book. Good luck!"

Top 10 Points About Real Estate Investing

1. Real estate investing is a great way to make a lot of money – but it is not risk-free and it is not easy.

2. Real estate investing is a very active endeavor.

3. Real estate investing is for people who like to sell.

4. Asking prices are meaningless.

5. The methodology of analysis of a real estate investment is the same whatever the type of property.

6. If you can't figure out a way to add value, pass on the deal.

7. There are many ways to add value – in all cases the goal is to boost the value of your property by multiples of what you invest.

8. Leverage is an important part of increasing your return on investment.

9. Understanding how to raise capital from partners will increase the number and size of the deals you can do.

10. Don't go into real estate just to get rich. There are easier ways to lose money.

1. REAL ESTATE IS A GREAT WAY TO MAKE A LOT OF MONEY – BUT IT IS NOT RISK FREE AND IT IS NOT EASY.

I personally hate the promoters who are selling real estate dreams. My guess is that some of them have never even done a successful real estate deal.

Anyone who has made a lot of money as a real estate investor has learned the hard way that there are ups and downs in the business. Certainly the game is to have more ups than downs, but all of us who have been in the business for any period of time are very respectful of risk. Not every factor in a deal can be controlled. Sometimes an investor is simply subject to forces beyond his or her control.

2. REAL ESTATE INVESTING IS A VERY ACTIVE ENDEAVOR.

Unlike putting your money into more passive vehicles like stocks or bonds and then hoping you made a good buy, real estate ownership allows you to roll up your sleeves and influence what happens after you buy.

There are many ways for the active investor to improve the value of his investment...here are four examples:

1. Better control of the operating costs of the property
2. Better rental program – to increase rents
3. Aggressive leasing program – to lease vacancies
4. Better management – keep your existing tenants happy

3. REAL ESTATE INVESTING IS FOR PEOPLE WHO LIKE TO SELL.

Real estate investing is not high-tech. It is not complicated math. It is not brain surgery.

It is about salesmanship. About convincing a seller to sell to you at a price that makes sense. About convincing a lender to loan you money. About convincing partners to invest with you. About convincing tenants to lease in your property. About convincing a buyer to buy your building after you have added value.

The best real estate investors know how to sell ... they usually have excellent "people skills."

4. ASKING PRICES ARE MEANINGLESS.

Some real estate investors get into trouble because they work within the framework of the seller's asking price. As far as I am concerned a seller can ask for the moon but if the numbers do not work, I pass. In fact, part of my goal as a real estate investor is to educate a seller why his number is not realistic and convince him that no buyer will pay his asking price. In these situations I suggest that he may as well deal with me if he wants to sell his property.

5. THE METHODOLOGY OF ANALYSIS OF A REAL ESTATE INVESTMENT IS THE SAME WHATEVER THE TYPE OF PROPERTY.

The cash-flow analyses we did in this book are indicative of what one does whether buying a small, single-family house to lease out or, a 1,000,000 square foot office building. In all cases we are trying to isolate projected gross rents, operating costs, and net operating income. Then, after we deduct debt payments we derive what is often called cash flow.

The cash flow divided by your investment (equity) in the deal equals your return on investment.

6. IF YOU CAN'T FIGURE OUT A WAY TO ADD VALUE, PASS ON A DEAL.

I do not believe in buying a deal which has no added value opportunity. I don't pursue deals that depend upon rents to gradually increase over time. Sometimes rents do increase (usually due to supply and demand) but sometimes they fall. The type of investor who buys a deal with no added value opportunities is usually an institutional investor who does not have the entrepreneurial mind set or creativity to add value.

7. THERE ARE MANY WAYS TO ADD VALUE.

The point of adding value is to look for ways that you can boost your net operating income – hopefully, dramatically and quickly.

For example, perhaps you have found an older building for sale that does not show well given its run-down appearance. Sometimes just with moderate renovation (for example, cosmetics), the leasing market starts to take notice of a building and sees it in a new way. This improved visage can translate to higher rents!

8. LEVERAGE IS AN IMPORTANT PART OF INCREASING YOUR RETURN.

One of the keys to success with real estate investing is learning how to use borrowed money. Like a lever which allows you to move objects too heavy to move by yourself, borrowed money allows you to achieve a return much higher than you would without borrowed money.

As we saw in our analyses above, using borrowed money improved the return dramatically.

9. UNDERSTANDING HOW TO RAISE CAPITAL FROM PARTNERS WILL INCREASE THE NUMBER AND SIZE OF THE DEALS YOU CAN DO.

If you believe in a purchase and are willing to put in some of your own money and, you can sell others on your vision for the deal, you will find people willing to invest with you. As your deal performs, people will want to go into your future deals, which will broaden the spectrum of the type and size of deals you can do.

10. DON'T GO INTO REAL ESTATE UNLESS YOU ENJOY THE PROCESS. THERE ARE EASIER WAYS TO LOSE MONEY.

As with anything, if you are in an activity JUST for the money, you are probably not going to be very successful.

Since real estate investing can be risky, if you are not committed to an active, engaged role with your properties, you are taking unnecessary chances with your financial well-being.

There are easier ways to lose money than real estate investing.

CONCLUSION

Real estate investing can be an exhilirating and very profitable endeavor. But, it is neither risk-free, nor easy. It is, in fact, challenging. However, the principles for success are actually fairly basic. After you learn them, it is all about execution.

We at **The Skinny On**™ hope that you have enjoyed our book. As always, we would love to hear from you.

With warm regards,

Jim Randel
jrandel@theskinnyon.com